Backyard Bugs & Creepy Crawlies

Spiders

Ava Podmorow

e Explore other books at:
WWW.ENGAGEBOOKS.COM

VANCOUVER, B.C.

ℯ→ WWW.ENGAGEBOOKS.COM

Spiders: Level Pre-1
Backyard Bugs & Creepy Crawlies
Podmorow, Ava 2004 –
Text © 2022 Engage Books
Design © 2022 Engage Books

Edited by: A.R. Roumanis
and Sarah Harvey

Text set in Epilogue

FIRST EDITION / FIRST PRINTING

LIBRARY AND ARCHIVES CANADA CATALOGUING IN PUBLICATION

Title: Spiders / Ava Podmorow.
Names: Podmorow, Ava, author.
Description: Series statement: Backyard bugs & creepy-crawlies
Engaging readers: level pre-1, beginner.

Identifiers: Canadiana (print) 20220403414 | Canadiana (ebook) 20220403422
ISBN 978-177476-704-7 (hardcover)
ISBN 978-177476-705-4 (softcover)
ISBN 978-177476-706-1 (epub)
ISBN 978-177476-707-8 (pdf)

Subjects:
LCSH: Spiders—Juvenile literature.

Classification: LCC QL452.2 .P63 2022 | DDC J595.4/4—DC23

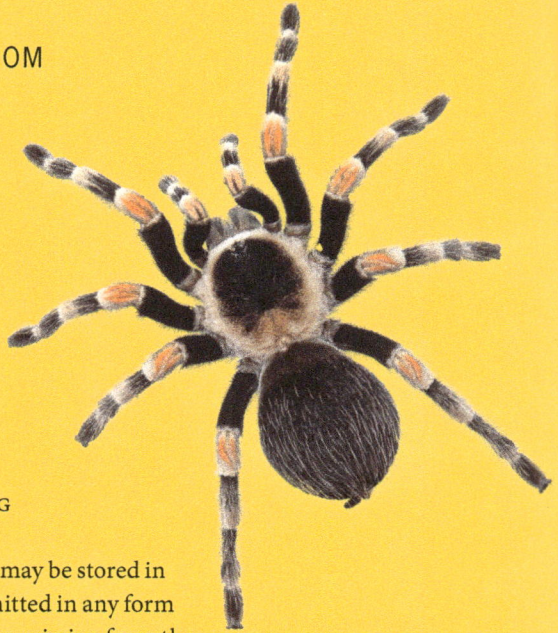

This project has been made possible in part
by the Government of Canada.

Canada

Spiders are not insects!

Spiders have 8 legs.
Insects have 6 legs.

Legs

Some spiders
have no eyes.
Some have
up to 8 eyes.

Eyes

There are over 45,000 kinds of spiders in the world.

Eight-spotted Crab Spider

Spiders do not
like the cold.

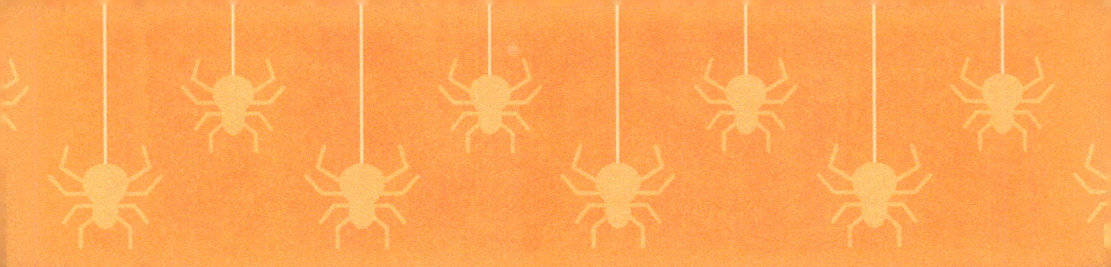

They live near buildings to stay warm.

Some spiders live in and on water.

Great Raft Spider

They can run on
top of the water.

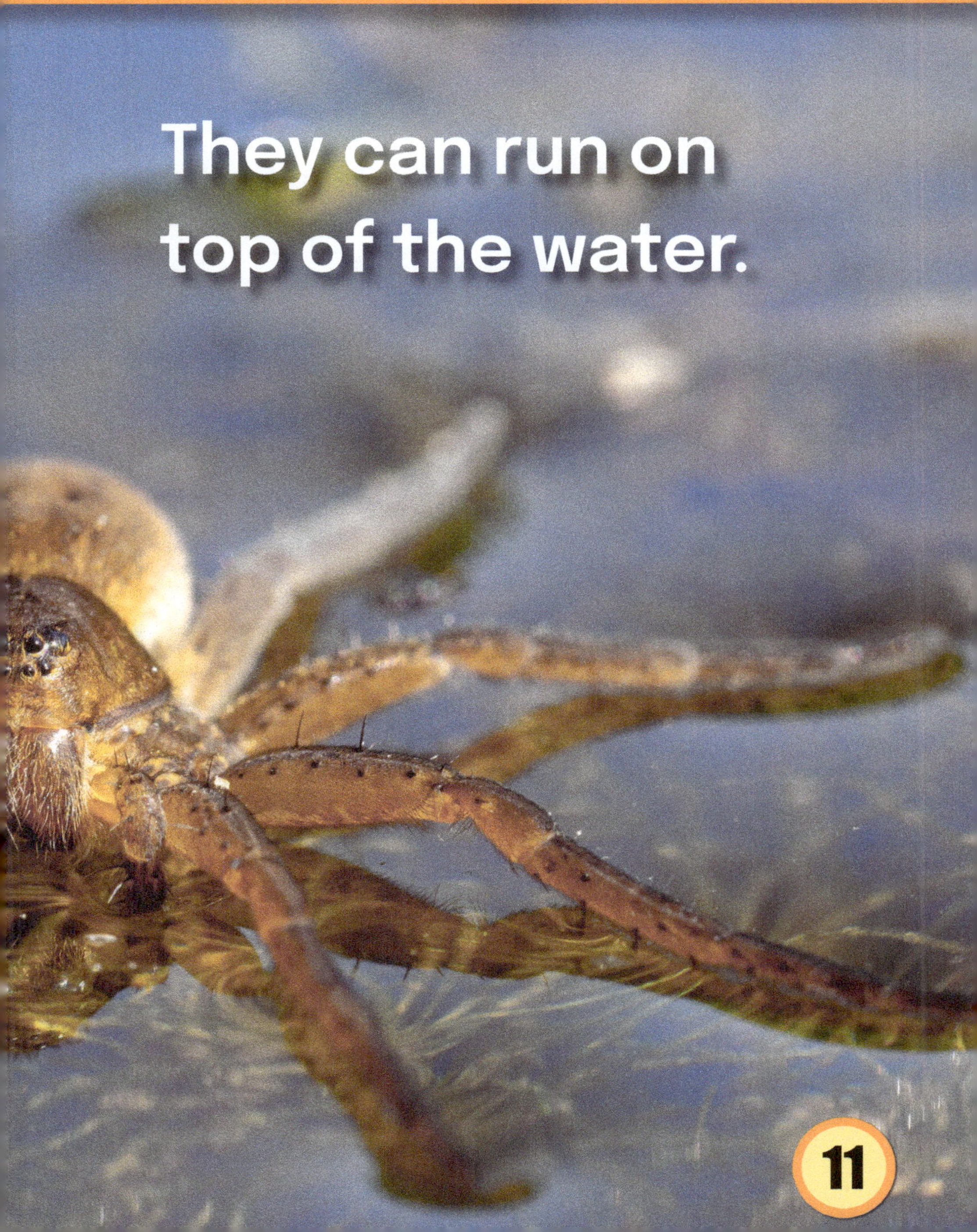

A spider feels things better than it sees them.

Jumping Spider

13

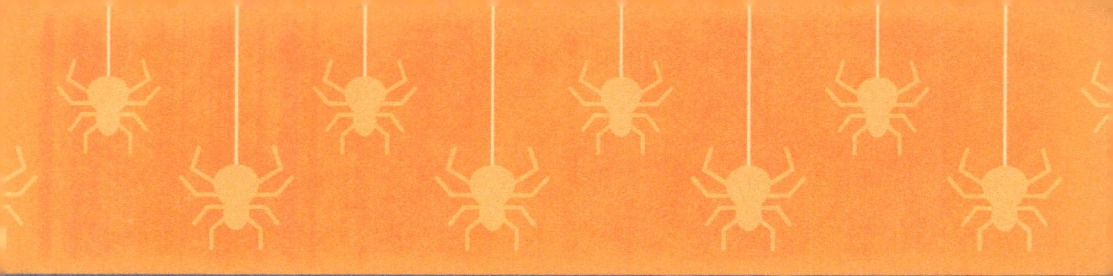

Female

Female spiders are usually much larger than male spiders.

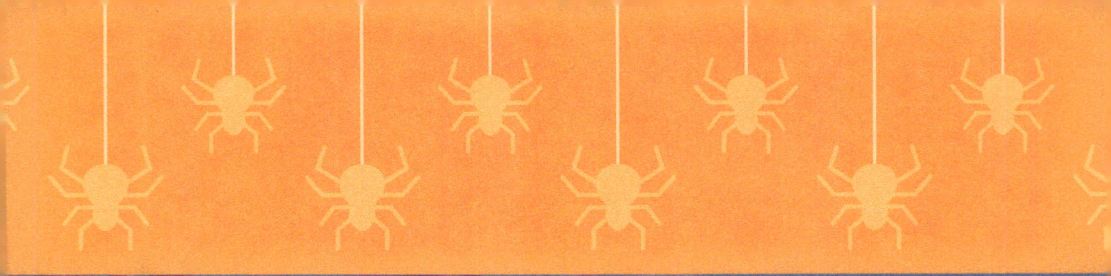

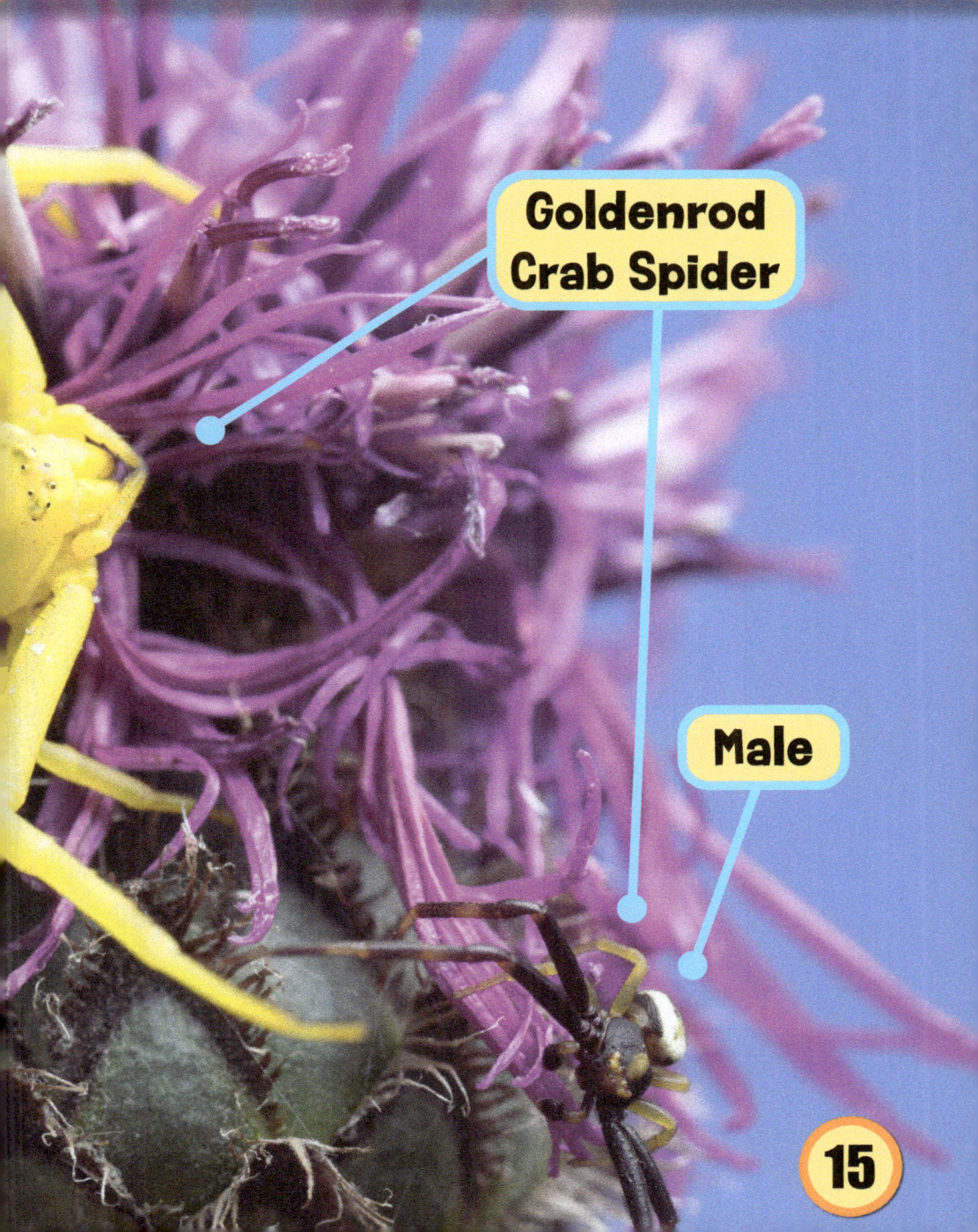

Goldenrod Crab Spider

Male

Female spiders can have 2 to 1,000 babies at a time!

Baby Spiders

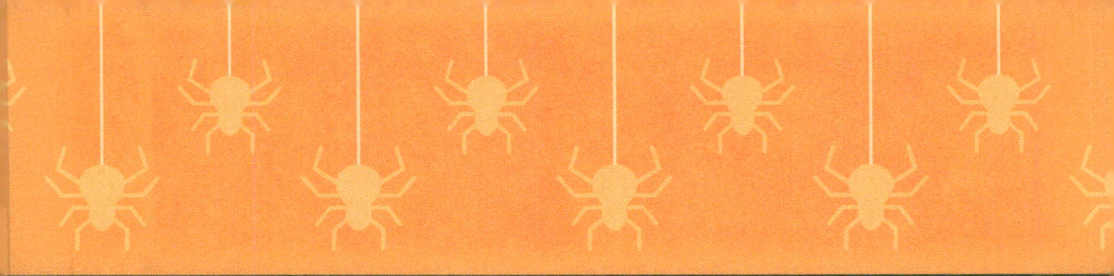

Wolf Spider

Spider babies start out as eggs.

The eggs hatch when the weather is warm.

Some spiders make webs. They push a silky string out of their bodies.

Spiders use their webs to catch food. They eat flies, grasshoppers, and even other spiders.

Grasshopper

This helps keep
Earth healthy.

23

Spiders use their fangs to eat.

Fangs

Some spiders can be kept as pets.

Tarantula

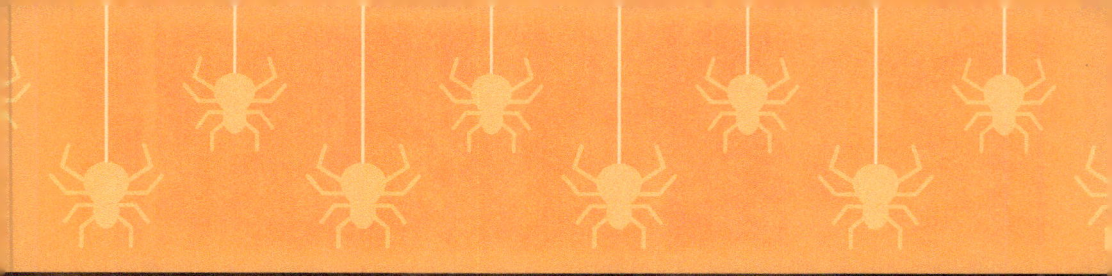

Many people are afraid of spiders.

Explore other books in the Backyard Bugs & Creepy Crawlies series!

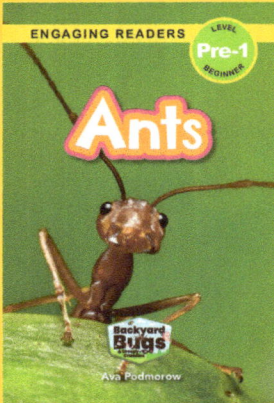

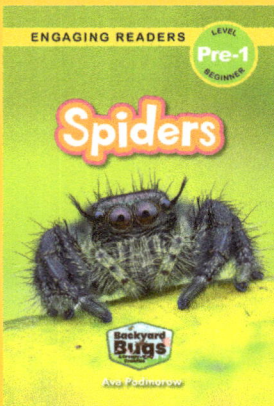

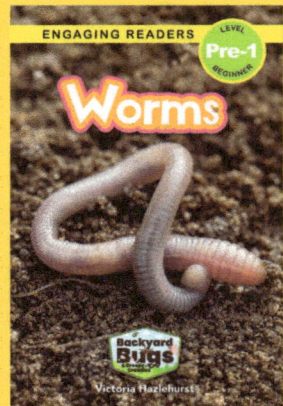

ENGAGING READERS — LEVEL Pre-1 BEGINNER
Ants
Backyard Bugs
Ava Podmorow

ENGAGING READERS — LEVEL Pre-1 BEGINNER
Beetles
Backyard Bugs
Victoria Hazlehurst

ENGAGING READERS — LEVEL Pre-1 BEGINNER
Caterpillars
Backyard Bugs
Ava Podmorow

ENGAGING READERS — LEVEL Pre-1 BEGINNER
Grasshoppers
Backyard Bugs
Ava Podmorow

ENGAGING READERS — LEVEL Pre-1 BEGINNER
Moths
Backyard Bugs
Ava Podmorow

ENGAGING READERS — LEVEL Pre-1 BEGINNER
Snails
Backyard Bugs
Ava Podmorow

ENGAGING READERS — LEVEL Pre-1 BEGINNER
Spiders
Backyard Bugs
Ava Podmorow

ENGAGING READERS — LEVEL Pre-1 BEGINNER
Wasps
Backyard Bugs
Sarah Harvey

ENGAGING READERS — LEVEL Pre-1 BEGINNER
Worms
Backyard Bugs
Victoria Hazlehurst

Visit www.engagebooks.com/readers

Explore books in the Animals In The City series.

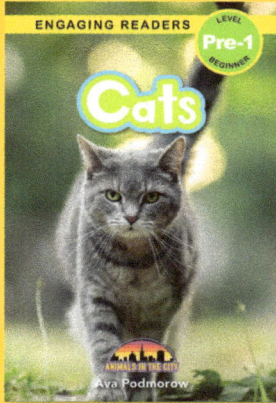

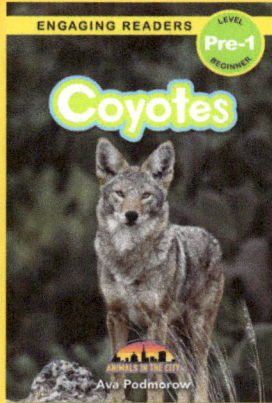

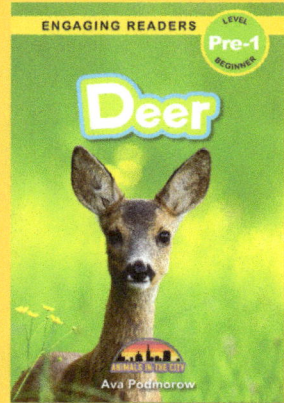

ENGAGING READERS — LEVEL Pre-1 BEGINNER
Cats
ANIMALS IN THE CITY
Ava Podmorow

ENGAGING READERS — LEVEL Pre-1 BEGINNER
Coyotes
ANIMALS IN THE CITY
Ava Podmorow

ENGAGING READERS — LEVEL Pre-1 BEGINNER
Deer
ANIMALS IN THE CITY
Ava Podmorow

ENGAGING READERS — LEVEL Pre-1 BEGINNER
Owls
ANIMALS IN THE CITY
Ava Podmorow

ENGAGING READERS — LEVEL Pre-1 BEGINNER
Pigeons
ANIMALS IN THE CITY
Ava Podmorow

ENGAGING READERS — LEVEL Pre-1 BEGINNER
Rabbits
ANIMALS IN THE CITY
Ava Podmorow

ENGAGING READERS — LEVEL Pre-1 BEGINNER
Raccoons
ANIMALS IN THE CITY
Sarah Harvey

ENGAGING READERS — LEVEL Pre-1 BEGINNER
Rats
ANIMALS IN THE CITY
Ava Podmorow

ENGAGING READERS — LEVEL Pre-1 BEGINNER
Skunks
ANIMALS IN THE CITY
Ava Podmorow

Visit www.engagebooks.com/readers